WELCOME

A MONASTIC COMMUNITY IN DEVON

Buckfast Abbey is a Benedictine monastery, on the edge of Dartmoor, that is visited by almost half a million people a year. Visitors come for both the tranquil atmosphere and inspirational story surrounding St Mary's Abbey, as well as the rare opportunity to encounter a Roman Catholic monastic community.

The first Abbey was founded in 1018 and absorbed into the Cistercian order in 1147. It grew throughout the Middle Ages until its closure in 1539 by King Henry VIII. The buildings were converted or allowed to fall into ruin, but in 1882 a group of Benedictine monks, exiled from France, settled at Buckfast and eventually set about rebuilding the Abbey. It now seems incredible that a team of no more than six monks completed the work in 30 years, especially as only one – Brother Peter – had any experience as a builder. This feat was made possible by their unshakeable determination to build a lasting symbol of monastic heritage and a living community dedicated to following the Benedictine Rule.

Today Buckfast Abbey is the only English medieval monastery to have been restored and used again for its original purpose. The monks here pray and work in the exact spot and in the same ways that their predecessors did nearly a thousand years ago. They follow the guidelines that were set down by their founder, St Benedict, in the fifth century, and they continue to support themselves through a variety of means, including the traditional monastic occupations of beekeeping, land management, wine production and hospitality.

Visitors are welcome in the church, grounds and outer buildings, although the monastic enclosure is private.

SHORT HISTORY OF BUCKFAST ABBEY

FROM THE ELEVENTH TO THE TWENTY-FIRST CENTURY

*B*uckfast Abbey was founded in 1018. Built from wood, the Saxon Abbey was smaller and less prosperous than many of England's other monasteries. Its endowments were recorded in 1086 in the Domesday survey – 300 acres at Buckfast and nearly 10,000 acres across 13 manors elsewhere in the region, which supported tenants and livestock.

BELOW: A 1734 print records the state of the ruined Abbey before it was finally demolished early in the nineteenth century to make way for William Berry's new mansion.

THE EAST VIEW OF BUCKFASTRE-ABBY, IN THE COUNTY OF DEVON.

Bocfast, Bucfastre, or Buckfastleigh, was an Abbey of White Monks of the Cistercian Order, dedicated to the blessed Virgin, some say it was originally Founded by Duke Alfred before the Conquest. And others Attribute it to Ethelward son of Wm. de Pomeroy, in the time of H.H.II. tis certain this King, confirm'd its Grants & Priveleges; Among its principal Benefactors, was Rich. Banzan, who endow'd them with certain Lands to hold by the 30th part of a Knights Fee. — Annual Value according to Dugdale. £466-11-2. I.& N. Buck delin et Sculp.1734.

Reproduced by A. Wheaton & Co. Ltd. for Devon Books, 1984.

1018
Land is cleared and the first Abbey is founded.

1086
The Domesday survey records the Abbey's property.

1147
King Stephen gives the Abbey to Cistercian monks, who rebuild it completely.

1215
King John names the Abbot of Buckfast as custodian of the crown jewels.

1297
King Edward I stays at the Abbey 8–10 April.

1539
The Abbey is dissolved and given to King Henry VIII – lands are sold and buildings fall into ruin.

The early monks would have followed the *Regularis Concordia* – a rule of life that was drawn up to re-establish and invigorate monastic life. After Domesday the Abbey appears to have entered a period of decline that lasted until the reign of King Stephen. He sought to revive English monasteries, first by bringing them under the rule of the new Abbey of Savigny in southern Normandy, but 11 years later all the Savigniac houses were absorbed into the Cistercian Order. The arrival of the Cistercians at Buckfast in 1147 was part of the rapid expansion of their centralised order (see pages 4–5) and brought immediate transformation – the whole monastery was rebuilt in stone along the Cistercian pattern.

In the fourteenth century Buckfast Abbey was struck by the Black Death, and some of the buildings fell into disuse for about 30 years. By the fifteenth century, however, the Cistercian monastery had recovered its vigour. The Monks continued to uphold their social responsibilities by overseeing parishes and manors, establishing fairs and markets to encourage local trade, welcoming visitors and running a monastic school.

By the beginning of the sixteenth century Europe's monasteries were in decline. They had been eclipsed by the universities as centres of learning, while secular hospitals and inns were increasing at the expense of those run by monasteries. Meanwhile a diminishing number of monks and nuns owned a larger share of property and tithes.

In 1535 Henry VIII, who was in debt from expensive overseas campaigns, ordered a detailed survey of ecclesiastical property. His break from Rome in the 1536 Act of Supremacy gave him control of England's monasteries, which he quickly dissolved. Buckfast Abbey was closed on 25 February 1539, falling into ruin until it was converted into a four-turreted mansion by a local mill owner, William Berry.

In 1882 exiled French Benedictine monks settled at Buckfast, and this community eventually decided to rebuild the Cistercian monastery. From their return until the present day this modern community has followed the same Rule as their medieval predecessors. Into the new century the monks have cared for the Abbey, their own community and the wider world.

LEFT: The Guest House (a nineteenth-century mansion built on the site of the medieval monastery) is part of the re-built Monastery. It houses visitors' rooms and the Parish office.

1806
A gothic-style mansion is built using stone from the Abbey's ruins.

1882
Thirty French Benedictine monks come to Buckfast and decide to rebuild the Abbey.

1906
Abbot Natter is drowned at sea. His successor, Anscar Vonier, determines to rebuild the Abbey.

1938
Rebuilding of the Abbey is completed.

1968
The Blessed Sacrament Chapel within the Abbey Church is built.

GROWTH IN THE MIDDLE AGES

THE CISTERCIAN ORDER AT BUCKFAST

The Cistercian order was conceived as a return to the Rule of St Benedict in its original, pure form – shirts, bedspreads and robes were banned along with all 'luxuries', and churches were stripped of all 'ornament'; the rule of silence and vegetarian diet were reaffirmed. The Cistercian monks, helped by lay-brothers, were dedicated to prayer and work, mostly on their estates, which were often in isolated and inhospitable places. In this way, they cleared and drained huge tracts of land and developed Europe's wool trade. The Cistercian order expanded rapidly, reaching Buckfast in 1147.

This early manuscript shows Cistercian monks arriving at the Abbey of Clairvaux. Taken from the Chronicles of the Kings and Dukes of Burgundy (French, 1485-90).

The Benedictine Rule

St Benedict (born 480 AD) wrote 'This little Rule for beginners' to help monks draw closer to God. His Rule was a combination of ideals and practical rules governing all aspects of community life. By following this Rule, over centuries monks have developed a well-rounded daily routine of prayer, study and work in the context of a stable, caring community life.

A statue of St Benedict in the chapel dedicated to his memory within The Abbey Church.

A Monk's Vows

From the Rule emerged three distinct vows, which are taken by those entering Benedictine monasteries like Buckfast to this day:

Stability – a commitment to live and work in a particular community for the rest of one's life.

Obedience – to put God and the community before oneself; in the first instance a monk's obedience is to the Abbot.

Conversion of Life – to grow spiritually within the community; this is seen as a life-long process.

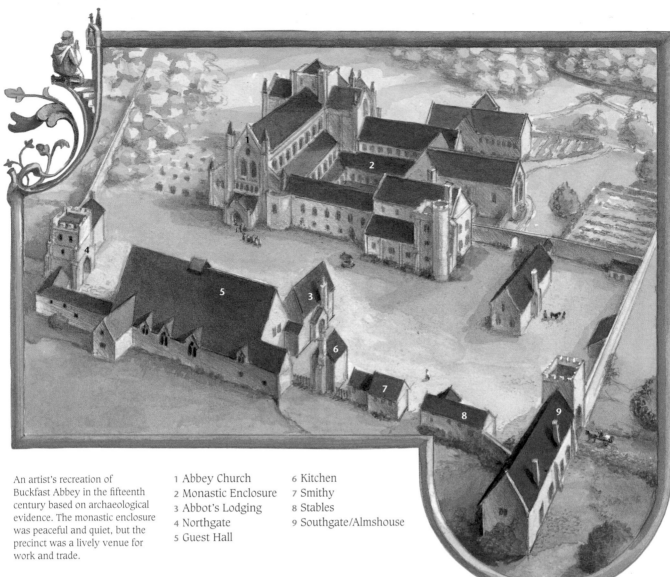

An artist's recreation of Buckfast Abbey in the fifteenth century based on archaeological evidence. The monastic enclosure was peaceful and quiet, but the precinct was a lively venue for work and trade.

1 Abbey Church
2 Monastic Enclosure
3 Abbot's Lodging
4 Northgate
5 Guest Hall
6 Kitchen
7 Smithy
8 Stables
9 Southgate/Almshouse

LEFT: The surviving arch of Northgate nearby the Grange Restaurant. This was the main entrance to the precinct in the Middle Ages.

RIGHT: This enamelled bookplate and jewelled cross from the medieval Abbey were discovered during excavations of the grounds.

After its change of ownership, Buckfast Abbey was rebuilt in stone along the Cistercian pattern. The new church was positioned in an east-west direction, and it was joined at the south by a monastic enclosure. Both buildings were in the centre of a precinct that had gates to the north and south for travellers to enter through. Monasteries fulfilled an important role by providing hospitality, and Buckfast Abbey was on the packhorse route that carried trade through the region. By the fifteenth century its buildings had been added to with a Guest Hall for travellers to stay in, a luxurious Abbot's Lodging for important visitors and a separate Almshouse for the needy.

COMMUNITY LIFE

FOLLOWING THE RULE FROM THE MIDDLE AGES TO THE TWENTY-FIRST CENTURY

from the arrival of the Cistercians to the dissolution of their monastery at Buckfast, the routine of the monks remained unchanged day to day and for centuries as they followed the Rule of St Benedict, which valued prayer, work, study and the care of others. Today, monks and nuns around the world follow the same pattern of life as their predecessors. This is not from any desire to recreate the past, but simply because the Rule is as relevant today as ever, and easily adaptable to the conditions of time and place.

ABOVE: The Abbot's Tower is a surviving portion of the medieval monastery.

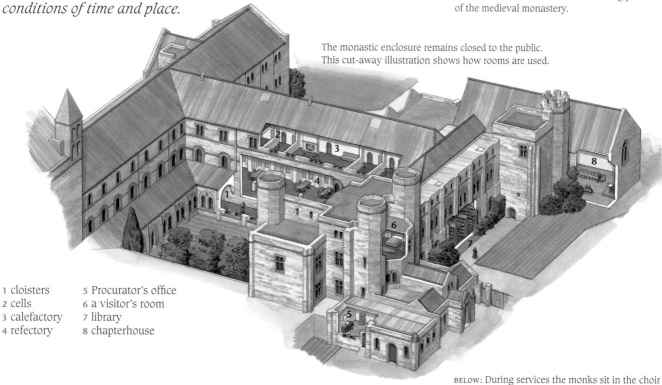

The monastic enclosure remains closed to the public. This cut-away illustration shows how rooms are used.

1 cloisters
2 cells
3 calefactory
4 refectory
5 Procurator's office
6 a visitor's room
7 library
8 chapterhouse

BELOW: During services the monks sit in the choir stalls and chant or sing from the Book of Psalms.

Daily Timetable

5.45am Service – Matins (morning prayer)
6.15am Private prayer
6.45am Service – Lauds
7.00am Breakfast
8.00am Service – Mass
9.00am Work
1.00pm Service – Midday prayer
1.15pm Lunch
2.00pm Work
6.15pm Chapter meeting
6.30pm Service – Vespers (evening prayer)
7.00pm Spiritual reading
7.30pm Supper
8.00pm Free time
9.00pm Service – Compline (night prayer)

St Benedict placed great importance on the communal performance of a series of services – the Divine Office. He called this the Work of God and instructed that 'nothing must be put before' it.

To this day prayer and the worship of God, by which we give thanks for the many benefits we enjoy and place ourselves within the loving embrace of God, is central to the lives of monks. The pattern of worship has changed slightly – the monks now celebrate mass jointly before a congregation, and all services are held in the Abbey Church.

'The Abbot should always realise ... that to whom more is entrusted, more is required.' And 'he should arrange everything with foresight and fairness.'

St Benedict believed that monasteries should be organised fairly. The monks elected their Abbot, and in the Middle Ages he held the position for life. In this tradition, the Abbot is still voted for by the other monks, although he is now elected for 8 years rather than for life. Today the monks also cast votes on issues affecting their community, which are presented to them by the Abbot during Chapter meetings. Every monk is allowed to speak at these meetings, and voting is carried out by a secret ballot. Monks are also fully involved in the day-to-day running of the Abbey's industries and facilities alongside dedicated lay staff.

A Guest Master welcomes visitors to the monastery, and lay brothers lead the horses away to the stables.

Today, a granite stone cross is a feature of the precinct. It is one of the many crosses that mark the ancient route across Dartmoor from Buckfast Abbey to another abbey at Tavistock, some 23 miles away. An annual walk takes place along this route – now known as the Abbot's Way – on the first Sunday of October.

'The vice of personal ownership must by all means be cut out in the monastery by the very root, so that no one may presume to ... have anything whatever as his own, neither a book, nor a writing tablet, nor a pen.'

Throughout the centuries, on joining a monastery, monks have relinquished the right to hold personal property and instead worked for the Abbey and shared in its fortunes. By wearing identical habits, eating the same food (and in the middle ages sleeping in a dormitory), monks have expressed their unwavering commitment to the Buckfast community.

'Let all guests that come be received like Christ, for he will say: "I was a stranger and you took me in". And let fitting honour be shown to all.'

Then as now hospitality was central to life at Buckfast Abbey. The monks welcomed pilgrims, travellers and merchants as they passed through or stayed at the monastery. Records indicate that in 1297 King Edward I stayed at the Abbey with a large retinue of soldiers, servants, courtiers and advisors.

A Sacristan prepares the altar, which has a silver cross and candlesticks.

Archaeological evidence has also revealed that the Guest Hall was one of the largest in England; today the Abbey Bookshop is housed there, but the building would once have been double its present height and width. The tradition of hospitality is continued in a number of guesthouses for those wishing 'to get away from it all', a conference centre and not least facilities for about 400,000 visitors a year.

'Idleness is the enemy of the soul ... then are they truly monks when they live by the labour of their hands.'

St Benedict believed that hard work was a monk's duty to God and his community. At Buckfast the monks farmed the manorial lands and tended the gardens in the Abbey's precinct, providing food for their own table and produce that could be sold in nearby markets. With the River Dart running close by, fishing was another important activity, and in the Abbey's infirmary, library and workshops the monks would have dedicated themselves to the pursuits of medicine, scholarship and craftsmanship.

PRODUCTS OF BUCKFAST ABBEY

HONEY, STAINED GLASS AND TONIC WINE

*J*n the Middle Ages monasteries were supported by rents from their lands, but the monks who returned to Buckfast relied on other ways of being self-sufficient. They produced their own food and made different wares for sale, the most successful of which has been tonic wine. The Abbey also specialises in bee keeping, as well as the art of stained glass.

In the Middle Ages, basketwork hives were set in to 'bee boles', which are still visible in the ancient walls of the Abbey. Today, Buckfast honey is produced in over 200 hives distributed around the Abbey grounds and local farms and orchards.

Beekeeping at Buckfast dates back to the Middle Ages. In an ancient wall near Southgate, visitors can see a line of 'bee boles' – recesses for basketwork hives. Known to beekeepers all over the world, the Buckfast bee™ was developed by Brother Adam, who contributed more than 70 years of his life to beekeeping at Buckfast Abbey. His long career was spent breeding a new kind of bee that was disease-resistant, gentle and, above all, a good honey producer. Buckfast bees are bred in isolation in the centre of Dartmoor. Honey is produced in over 200 hives distributed around the Abbey grounds, local farms and orchards. In season, Buckfast honey can be purchased in the Abbey's Gift Shop, but it is very popular and sells out quickly!

The magnificent stained-glass window of the Last Supper, which dominates the Blessed Sacrament Chapel at the east end of the Abbey Church, was created by the late Father Charles Norris. He trained at the Royal College of Art and developed a modern style of stained glass by using thick tiles of glass, which were chipped to shape and set in concrete or epoxy resins. Over the last 50 years, the monks of Buckfast Abbey have designed and produced windows for over 150 churches, as well as many private commissions. One notable recent commission was a window for a memorial in

ABOVE: Visiting school children admire stained glass in the Chapel of the Blessed Sacrament.

LEFT: The window of the Last Supper is a load-bearing wall of large glass blocks, which have been chipped on the inside to refract the light from outside. It was designed and built by Dom Charles Norris.

New York to the firemen killed in the terrorist attack on the World Trade Centre on September 11 2001.

Wine making is another traditional monastic industry. Many of the great wines of Europe are results of the skill, ingenuity and hard work of monks. Perhaps the most famous of these is Dom Perignon, the inventor of Champagne. Buckfast has become famous for its Tonic Wine, the recipe for which was brought to Buckfast by the community, who re-founded the Abbey in 1882. First produced merely as a medicinal drink for domestic use, it was later marketed on a small scale to visitors who came to watch the rebuilding of the Abbey. In the 1920s changes to the licensing laws threatened its commercial production. J. Chandler Ltd. undertook to handle distribution and sale, and the monks continued to make tonic wine in the Abbey cellars. The tonic

LEFT: The recipe for tonic wine was brought to Buckfast by the monks who settled there in the 1880s. By the 1920s, when this photograph was taken, it was being produced in large quantities.

wine was changed slightly, from the rather severe patent medicine into a smoother, more mature medicated wine, and Buckfast Tonic Wine™ as we know it today was born. Buckfast Tonic Wine can be found for sale in both the Gift Shop and the Monastic Produce Shop and, indeed, some of the items in the Grange Restaurant contain Buckfast Tonic Wine (see pages 18–20).

DESTRUCTION & REBUILDING

AN INSPIRATIONAL STORY OF FAITH

Until 1535 there had been an unbroken line of abbots appointed by the monks, but in that year Gabriel Donne, a close friend of Thomas Cromwell, was imposed on the community. He laid the ground for the process of dissolution by selling off the Abbey's property until 25 February 1539, when two of the King's commissioners and a band of lawyers arrived to complete the closure. Buckfast Abbey was one of 40 West Country monasteries they visited and closed over just four months. At each they presented and witnessed the signing of the Deed of Surrender, then handed out pensions to the monks and took possession of their seals, charters and plate.

At Buckfast, the community was dispersed – five of the monks are known to have found employment in local parishes – and the lands were sold piecemeal and preferentially to people who were present at the Abbey's dissolution. The manor of Buckfast itself, including the Abbey, fell to Sir Thomas Dennys and remained in the Dennys family for 250 years. Demolition work began immediately – lead was melted down; moveables were auctioned off; a massive wooden crane was used to dismantle the roof

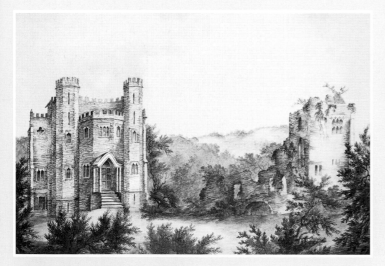

ABOVE: An 1825 water colour shows the mansion (left) and the Abbot's Tower (right). The space between these buildings would be filled during rebuilding of the Monastery in the twentieth century.

Buckfast Abbey has a rich archive of photographs that document the rebuilding of the Church and Monastery by a small team of monks, who used rudimentary tools and wooden scaffolding.

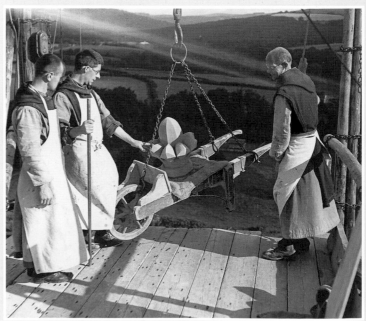

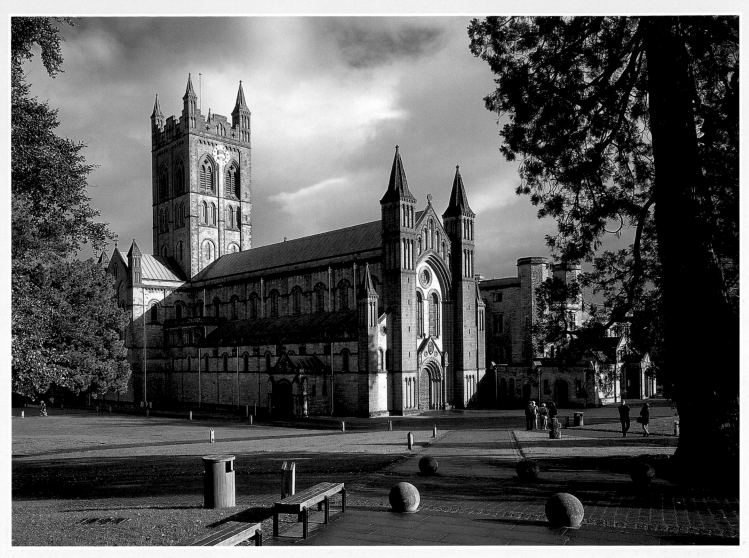

The outside walls of the rebuilt Church are made of local blue limestone; the window arches, quoins, coping stones and turrets are in mellow Ham Hill stone.

timbers; and the shell of the monastery was left to crumble. The smaller outer buildings in the precinct were converted for different uses – the Almshouse was used for wool dyeing (in large stone vats that were installed inside); the Guest Hall and associated buildings were converted into cottages and a farm.

During the eighteenth century the ruined Abbey was illustrated by artists, who saw it as romantic. In 1800 it was bought as a ruin by Samuel Berry, owner of a mill by Southgate, who used it to build a gothic-style mansion, which was completed in 1806. Victorian paintings show how much the view had changed over a few years – only the Abbot's Tower and twelfth-century undercroft had survived Berry's development. The new mansion changed hands four times before 1882, when it was advertised in *The Tablet* as 'a grand acquisition could it be restored to

its original purpose'. This came to the attention of a group of exiled Benedictine monks living in Ireland. Having fled from persecution in France, these monks were looking for a safe new home. They lost no time in moving to Buckfast and purchasing the Abbey for £4,700.

Some time after their return, the monks decided to rebuild the medieval Abbey. They appointed an architect, Frederick Walters, who first used the evidence of the 1734 print until the real foundations of the monastery were uncovered, enabling Walters to deduce the shape and height of the original structure. He also added features from more substantial Cistercian ruins, such as pointed windows and rounded arches, to the design.

After the tragic drowning of Abbot Natter, his successor – Anscar Vonier – announced that the rebuilding would proceed. Using a horse-and-cart and

stone from a nearby quarry, a small band of monks (normally four, and never more than six) undertook this massive task. Funds were low at first, so the monks dressed the stone and mixed the mortar in self-built workshops, erected scaffolding from wooden poles lashed together with rope and chain and manually hoisted the stones. They built the walls from platforms 150 feet above the ground, without helmets or safety rails and buffeted by the weather.

The Abbey was consecrated on 25 August 1932, but there was still work to do. The tower was made taller to accommodate the church bells, the final stone was laid on 24 July 1937, and all building work was completed by December 1938. The builders hurried to finish in time for Abbot Anscar's return to Buckfast from an overseas journey. He died three weeks after seeing his dream of a fully restored Abbey Church made a reality.

THE ABBEY CHURCH OF ST MARY AT BUCKFAST

Central to every monastery is its church. It is here that monks gather for prayer at regular intervals throughout the day.

The Abbey Church of St Mary serves as a parish church as well, and local Catholics assemble here to worship as a parish community. The Abbey Church also provides a quiet and peaceful haven for individuals of all denominations and from many different backgrounds and places to spend time in personal prayer and contemplation. All of this makes St Mary's one of the most intensely used religious buildings in the region, with a regular programme of seven weekday services, all open to the public.

There is a separate illustrated guidebook to the Abbey Church.

Stained glass in the Abbey Church depicting the flight into Egypt.

The Lady Chapel in the North Transept.

The marble floors in the Sanctuary and Choir viewed from the Lantern Tower.

The altar of the Chapel of the Holy Cross in the South Transept, which commemorates the Crucifixion.

THE GARDENS OF BUCKFAST ABBEY

OPEN SPACES AND CORNERS OF CALM

The constantly evolving gardens of Buckfast Abbey provide a pleasant environment for visitors and monks alike. Modelled partly on medieval plans, the gardens have been planted simply and boldly to reflect the scale of the church and the unadorned character of the surrounding architecture. The gardens are separated into small, self-contained areas – the Lavender Garden, Sensory Garden and Physic Garden – which are surrounded by open spaces and wonderful trees that change with the seasons.

The Lavender Garden is just below the terrace of the Grange Restaurant. With 150 varieties, some difficult to grow, this garden shows the sheer diversity of colour, size and shape within the lavender genus. The plants are shaped into rounded domes, and in summer they fill the precinct with their scent, attracting bees and butterflies.

The shaped hedges of the Lavender Garden add definition to the Autumn landscape.

The Sensory Garden is designed around a fountain that feeds two gentle streams.

If you wander down the path leading from the Lavender Garden, with the Abbey to your right, you will reach the Sensory Garden on the left. Based on designs for medieval pleasure gardens, this garden will stimulate your senses through sight, smell, sound and touch. The sound of trickling water and fragrant flowers make it a peaceful corner of the grounds. Water trickles from the old cider press in the centre of the garden and flows through the garden. Circling the fountain is a chamomile seat, which is surrounded by a trellis of honeysuckle and fragrant white roses.

Between the Sensory Garden and the Abbey Church is the Physic Garden. This has over 200 plants that were common in the Middle Ages and cultivated by monks for many different uses. The plants are divided into four sections: culinary, household, medicinal and poisonous. The culinary section contains a mixture of herbs and vegetables. Among the well-known plants are different varieties of onion and garlic (all used in the Middle Ages to flavour food and as antibiotics). The less common plants include dock and skirret (once grown as vegetables) and the herb Woodruff (used to flavour liqueurs, wine and sorbets). The household section includes plants grown for use as dyes, scents and cleaning agents. For example, rosemary and pineapple sage were scattered indoors to mask smells, and different parts of meadowsweet were used to produce green, blue and black dyes. Plants in the medicinal section were grown by monks for treating the sick. They include feverfew (for headaches and migraines), agrimony (for coughs and colds), self-heal (for hypertension and conjunctivitis) and both chamomile and lavender (used as antiseptics).

On an island in a pond are the poisonous plants. Most of these had uses, but the monks also knew they could be harmful if used wrongly. Lovage can add taste to many dishes but should be avoided by pregnant women or people with kidney complaints. Rue is a powerful insecticide and a germicide for wounds, but its sap can produce a painful rash. Monkshood is one of the most potent plants in this section – it was used as an arrow-tip poison and a death drink for criminals in the Middle Ages.

The monks' private gardens are behind the Physic and Sensory Gardens and are not open to the public.

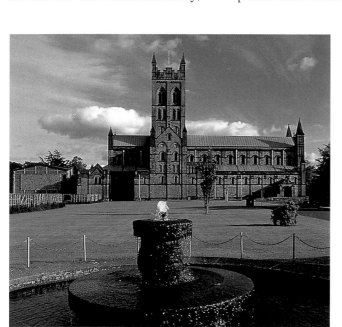

LEFT: Water trickles from Father Cuthbert's fountain outside the Conference Centre.

ABOVE RIGHT: Pink and yellow varieties of honeysuckle and Deep Secret roses fill the Sensory Garden with their scents.

RIGHT: The Physic Garden is divided into four sections containing plants grown by monks for their practical uses in the Middle Ages.

A TRADITION OF HOSPITALITY

VISITOR SERVICES AT BUCKFAST ABBEY

To the monks there is no conflict between their lifestyle and their welcoming visitors. Tourism is a way of 'living by the labour of their hands' and honouring St Benedict's rule of hospitality, while the money raised helps support the Abbey and enables it to undertake charitable and pastoral projects. In developing the precinct, the monks have sought to preserve the original fabric and function of its historic buildings, which are again available to visitors after centuries of neglect.

ABOVE: The restored Guest Hall (left) and Abbey bookshop (right) viewed from in front of the Abbey Church.

LEFT: The restored Guest Hall has an exterior stairway made out of wood from the Abbey's forests.

From the 1920s the Abbey, still under construction, began to attract visitors, whose imagination had been fired by the scale of the monks' work. Visitors' donations helped the rebuilding work to continue. As road and rail connections were improved, their numbers swelled. In 1932 the Great Western Railway even offered discounted fares for visitors to the Abbey. On the day of the Abbey's consecration, visitors filled the church and precinct, while radio and newspapers broadcast the occasion nationally, adding to the public's interest. By the 1970s Buckfast Abbey was among the West Country's most visited attractions. Facilities

had become outstretched, and fears of a 'never ending train of motor cars' expressed by villagers in the 1920s had become a reality. As a solution, the monks voted for a major redevelopment of the precinct.

Many hundreds of travellers would have stayed at the medieval **Guest Hall** (see pages 6–7), and by the early sixteenth century an addition had been built at right angles to the main hall. After the Dissolution, the Guest Hall became the property of a local farmer, who reduced the size of the main hall to suit his practical needs, and it was later converted into cottages. In 1983, the buildings were acquired by the

Buckfast Abbey Trustees who went on to approve a survey, which was the UK's largest, privately funded archaeological investigation at the time. This revealed the original size of the main hall (double its present height and width) and the unspoilt condition of the newer sixteenth-century hall, the appearance of which the Trustees decided to recreate.

The Guest Hall has been restored using oak from the Abbey's woods – the huge beams were manufactured on site, since every roof truss had to be made to size. Its cramped roof space and bare wood interior evoke its atmosphere as a working Guest Hall. The first floor would have been the main living area – today it contains a huge fireplace and recreated 'garde robe' (or open-seat toilet) – and all services were confined to the darker ground floor. Also visible inside are recesses that would have received the huge doors of the medieval Guest Hall and a window

surround that has been extended to show the sheer size of the original windows. On the outer west side are the ruins of the kitchen that supplied the Guest Hall. Archaeological investigations revealed the possibility of an external stairway to the first floor of the Guest Hall, and this has also been recreated with wood from the Abbey's woods.

South of the Guest Hall is the huge **Southgate**. In medieval times, this was the lesser of two arches through which travellers entered the precinct, but today it is the more impressive arch. At some stage the direction of the arch was altered, but further investigation is needed to discover the precise location of the original arch. Currently, the Southgate complex houses a retreat where both men and women can come to stay and experience the traditional timetable of monastic life. Southgate has been put to many uses over the centuries (almshouse, dyeing house and later a tenement), but, after being acquired by the Trustees in 1984, the whole building was gutted, and a major restoration project started. This opened up many of the features of the ancient building and created the modern retreat house of today.

A new addition was designed to be visibly distinct from the original building, and it was fitted with lifts and stairways to meet the requirements of a modern residential building. The ancient leat that once powered the higher mills was used to create a wonderful water garden, which provides an area for peaceful contemplation to be enjoyed by those staying at Southgate.

ABOVE: The Abbey bookshop is housed within the historic nooks and crannies of the former main hall of the medieval Guest Hall. It is one of the largest religious bookshops in the West Country.

BELOW: At the Southgate Retreat Centre people can share in the monastic round of services and the peace of the Abbey.

17

AROUND THE PRECINCT

The history of Buckfast is reflected in the buildings that make up the Abbey precinct. Like the Abbey itself, they cover a thousand-year span and have been adapted to changing influences and uses. Together, they tell a story of both change and continuity.

BELOW: These buildings to the north of the Abbey Church house the Conference Centre and Educational Activities Centre.

The ancient monastic tradition of education has been upheld by the monks of Buckfast Abbey. Soon after returning to Buckfast in the nineteenth century, they founded a village school. St Mary's Roman Catholic Primary School still operates in the village and attracts pupils from the surrounding parishes. In the 1960s, the monks also decided to form an independent, Roman Catholic, preparatory boarding school. Built to the north of the Abbey Church, this school operated successfully until boarding patterns changed, and it was closed in 1994. However, it is now used as a popular centre for conferences, training seminars and meetings. It also houses an award-winning, educational activities centre, which each year is visited by many thousands of school children. They can participate in hands-on activities, such as making arches, mosaics and stained-glass windows and even seeing how an organ works.

The Grange, which adjoins Northgate, was built in 1990 as a restaurant and tearooms. Like the medieval Guest Hall before it, The Grange now welcomes thousands of hungry and thirsty visitors to

Monastic in style, The Grange serves delicious hot and cold food to thousands of modern pilgrims.

Buckfast. Its architects were influenced by monastic tradition – the main serving area is reminiscent of the octagonal kitchen at Glastonbury Abbey, and the main eating area looks like a medieval tithe barn. The Grange was also designed with sympathy toward its surroundings – the ancient wall that leads from Northgate to Buckfast village has been incorporated into it.

Westgate, which contains an information centre, gift shop and toilets, was built in 1984. Its design was influenced by the gatehouse of another medieval monastery at Beaulieu in Hampshire. It was built to provide an entrance into the Abbey precinct from the car park, which was itself laid in 1983 to reduce car parking outside the Abbey Church. Although modern in style, Westgate has limestone walls, oak pillars and

ABOVE: Westgate presents an impressive entrance to the precinct and houses an information centre, gift shop and toilets.

RIGHT: The Methodist Chapel within the precinct is a place of shared worship for local Methodists and Anglicans.

a slate roof, enabling it to blend into its surroundings.

Nearby is a **Methodist Chapel**, and many people are puzzled by its presence in the Abbey precinct. When it was built in 1881 (a year before the monks returned to the monastery), this Chapel was situated on the main road of the village, which ran between the north and south gates. It is a testament to the strong influence of Wesleyanism in the area.

Passing through Westgate, one's eye is drawn towards the waterwheel on the Higher Mill. From the Middle Ages, the wool industry in Buckfast has been extremely important. Soft water, from the rivers Dart and Holy Brook, was used in the washing and dyeing of wool from sheep that were grazed on Dartmoor. In the early nineteenth century, the qualities of the water were recognised by William Berry, who built two new mills. The higher and lower mills were powered by a medieval leat running from the moors above the Abbey. The leat runs for approximately one and a half miles through a man-made watercourse and eventually over the wooden 'launder' (an overhead water way). Originally, this launder would have run through the Higher Mill to water turbines on the far side. When the mill was restored in 1995, the launder was truncated and allowed to drop over the current waterwheel (which was purpose built in Cornwall) into the small lake below. Over the centuries, the building has been put to many uses, but in 1988 it was acquired by the Trustees and converted for its current use with the agreement of English Heritage.

Housed within the Higher Mill, the Monastic Produce Shop sells wares of Buckfast Abbey, including tonic wine, fudge, honey, and other things made by monks and nuns from all over Europe.

LEFT: The Lower Mill is still used to produce wool. Passing through Southgate, visitors can go to this nearby viewing gallery and see the huge carding looms that produce quality wool for Axminster Carpets.

RIGHT: View of the Church tower.